Off The Heart

An Emotional Composition To The Dad's
Little Princess

Sowmya Venkataramany

India | USA | UK

Made with ❤ on the BookLeaf Publishing Platform
www.bookleafpub.in
www.bookleafpub.com

Dedication

It is the mother who brings the child with all that are required to be a responsible person in the society. She does everything. She goes to school with her kid as another kid itself. She does preparatories for all competitions, fancy dress, poems, elocution, essay writing, drawing and what not. She does the project work for the project of bringing her child. Only thing she doesn't is writing exam for her child since she is not allowed to do so.

This collection of emotions is nothing but the outcome of her inspiration. When she is not around reading these lines, droplets in the eyes proves this is "Off The Heart" and dedicate this to though departed but part of my heart, my beloved wife Mrs.Aswin Deepam Sowmya.

Preface

At the outset, I must say that I am not a poet but i am a father of my little princess. Every father in one way or other has to be part of writing such lines to his little princess when she forces him to do some for her to participate in her school competitions. I am also one of such father. The collections are nothing but expression of the love and only the love to be read and not between lines.

Acknowledgements

I sincerely acknowledge the schools in which my little princess studied as they are the instrumental to push me to coin these verses.

1. MOON

It's a day long wait
        To see this light
It comes in the night
        With the colour of white
It shines very bright
        But cool to the sight
It's reach is at height
        Even to the flight
But mummy invites
        For the baby's small bite
It comes down straight
        What a almight

2. HOLIDAY

Holiday is a Holiday

It's a day full of **H**appiness
     and happenings
It's a day full of **O**uting
     and eating
It's a day full of **L**eisure
     and pleasure
It's a day full of **I**nteraction
     and action
It's a day full of **D**ancing
     and singing
It's a day full of **A**musement
     and entertainment
It's a day full of **Y**elling
     and thrilling

It's a day full of fun
     and frolic

Holiday is a Holiday
Yeh! Yeh! Yeh!

3. My Progress Card

Dad was happy when the report card was shown
But not so happy, marks of history is lean
Arranged special class for history
It is as tough as writing poetry
What do I do, It's all about

"Before I born".

4. Ice Cream Wala

Bell rang, bell rang
We heard the bell ringing
We looked up and saw
It was the ice-cream wala.

Could not decide the choice of flavour
Whether Loo Loo or Laa Laa
At last decided the flavour Cocacola
Ho lallaa! Ho lallaa! Ho lallaa!

5. River

Its the river that flow
Breaks the rocks and blocks inflow
Carry the names of en-routes
But some water even glows
For it caters all without creeds
People of all ranks salutes
It's the rivers passion
Not to worry about identification
When becomes part of ocean.
Can anyone name its origination
But it is now part of Ocean
Everyone's destination
Ever Lasting.........Never Changing......

6. My School

It's a home away from home
Mummy guides and cares
Teachers give motherly care
Daddy is tuff, pulls me up
Mother gives me always pep
Lot of friends like kith and kins

We dine and dance
        after Maths and Science
Homework, classwork
        with a full of teamwork
Parents here builds the
        future

No compromise on culture
It's a home for 9 to 4

Yes, a home away from home

7. Leisure

Leisure time of mine
>is out of routine

It is the time for relaxation
>if used with passion

It is the time for deployment
>that gives enjoyment

It is not the free time
>time freed for firesome

It is the time for entertainment
>always come for attainment

Leisure gives pleasure
If used without pressure
>but with passion

8. My Family

My family is small
    but sweet
We are four
    but are one
Head is father
    also teacher
Mother is affectionate
    also strict
Brother is friendly
    all times
But fights at times

My family is small
    but sweet

9. The Train

The train runs fast in my sweet dream
I heard the sound cold ice-creams
Got the ticket for stage No.7,
Felt the travel like in the heaven
Opened the eyes, left my station
Yes, I screamed!

10. BUDDING POET

I sow the seed of thought
Pour the water of guidance,
Did the fence of support.

Waited the days of struggle,
Saw the light in the tunnel
Got the bright from the light
Grown with wings of leaves
Saw the budding today.

Poets are born - they say
They are made - I say
Yes! It's a budding poet

11. A Friends Choice

A friend of mine asked my choice
    to the deity
Snacks and rusks, biscuits and chocolates
    that are sweety
He told his choice to have lot of brains
Without which everything in on vain
What we don't have should ask
    the almighty

12. Diwali

This auspicious happened on Dwapar Yuga
Lord Krishna killed Naragasura
Celebrations still at every ghraha
With new clothes, sweets and kara
"Happy Diwali" at high pitch swara

People lit lights at home
Feels out, from dark and dream
Burns crackers with joy and fun
Cheers the day with kith and kin
Year long wait again back home!

13. HI GREED MANGO

I sow the seed of thought
Pour the water of guidance,
Did the fence of support
Waited the days of struggle,
Saw the light in the tunnel
Got the bright from the light.
Grown with wings of leaves
Saw the budding today.
Poets are born - they say
They are made - I say
Yes! It's a budding poet

14. NATURE

Nature is a God's gift to the Nation
It's a natural evolution
No place for duplication

It has green plantation
Beautiful hill station
Avoids air and other pollution

It gives togetherness sensation,
For the younger generation,
increases the concentration.

In the fast growing civilisation
Living with the nature,
Becomes an imagination

So let us do conservation
Of our natural vegetation
For the future generation

We are the creatures of the nature
Be with the creator, being a conservation
Don't be a seperator.

15. ROCK

Beware! Be with Nature

'NATURE', I am part of
          Natural to name me 'NATURE'
It is not I born
          Evolve and stand stubborn

Being helpful is my NATURE
          harming NATURE, human nurture
Thunder, storm, rain down pouring
          bearing, for human being
Beat me, hurt me with the hammer
          give them sand and stone for their shelter

Hill or valley, I do balance
          breaking cycle human paralance
Patience has its own tolerance
          Burst once to keep you silence

'NATURE', I am part of......
Beware! Be with NATURE

Aware! Human always mortal
          Can't win in NATURE'S battle

Since you are part of later
> See you not as different matter
No part is without a whole
> Be part of NATURE'S soul

'NATURE', I am part of......

16. RAIN

You come from nowhere
Can't spot where you are
Lived for short span
Gave life to everyone

Human life is too short
No point you looking back
Be helpful that you can
Lesson from rain you learn

17. EXAMINATION

Examination, A fear that lasts ever
Before joining, entrance fever
Goes on for entire year
A fear that lasts ever

Month on Month, it stops never
Eighties and Nineties though top scorer
Ten on ten parent's pressure
A fear that lasts ever.

Striving for good to better
Left out at last exam fever
Doctor says, do tests and exam
A fear that lasts ever.

18. SUPERMAN

To be strong enough to achieve goal
Just being strong, not enough;
To be brave enough to face the task.

Just being strong and brave
    not enough
Should be healthy enough to
    live long
Healthy without wealthy
    not enough

Having all could do nothing
If not kind and loveable
I could make myself of all above,
To help all around.

19. A Frog Came Down The Walk

A frog came down the walk
Looking for people to have a talk
It's hideout comes out from sounds it makes
People use it proverb sakes
But, I the saviour saved the frog in the park
When I knew it was going to be dark
Freakout time for venomous snake
We both took a walk around
Left it in backyard pond

20. War and Peace [Rose Vs Bee]

Once in a daw I went for jog
Breezy air and whitish fog
Flying birds singing mighty song
Joining hands, bell of church Ting Tong Tong

Eastern sky becomes bluish grey
The lighting star peeping into the day
Plants and trees dance the breezy' way
Horizon sky turned horsey bay

Rising sun blows its rays
Bour-Bon not known sign of ray
Buds of rose safe with sepals
Just born rose opens its petals

Petals with its bright in colour
Attracts the bees to this flower
Flying foe in search of honey
Sits and sucks in groups of many

Opened petals of Bour-Bon Rose
Couldn't be closed after sun rose
Knowing fully the powerful Sun

Couldn't stop this pitiful sin

Not to bear this
        War like act
Sun went and set
        On the west
Eating-up the Bour Bon feast
        Group of foe went for rest
Sacrificed his heart and soul
        Bour-Bon nodded in the night

This War and Peace of Bee and Rose
An act of latter's sacrifice
Sorry to say with what little knows
Love or Hatred God only knows

21. Be For Others To Be For Yourself

Lighting the incense spreads the fragrance
Sowing a seed feeds the Universe
Thy nurture the care and chracter
Maketh us to Shine and Glitter

To shine like a sea glass
Takes the travel to ages
Tide or Ebb it around turns
Gets the pebble to shine glass

Though doesn't shine or shaped
Tied together blogs of wood
Shines by it serves as a boat
To the fisher to have his feed

Bee goes on to blossom flower
Collects and stores tasteful nector
Fed us always with golden platter

Because of Thou we are here
Because of Thou we will be ever

Be by yourself thinking for others

You shine and makes others too
Tide and Ebb you only float
And makes people feel you great